About the Author

Mychaela lives in a small town in Illinois with her dog, Luna and her cat, Gertie. She is in the beginning stages of writing her second book and wishes to touch people's hearts that have been tarnished by life.

Pocket Love

Mychaela Frank

Pocket Love

Olympia Publishers
London

www.olympiapublishers.com
OLYMPIA PAPERBACK EDITION

Copyright © Mychaela Frank 2022

The right of Mychaela Frank to be identified as author of this work has been asserted in accordance with sections 77 and 78 of the Copyright, Designs and Patents Act 1988.

All Rights Reserved

No reproduction, copy or transmission of this publication may be made without written permission.
No paragraph of this publication may be reproduced, copied or transmitted save with the written permission of the publisher, or in accordance with the provisions of the Copyright Act 1956 (as amended).

Any person who commits any unauthorised act in relation to this publication may be liable to criminal prosecution and civil claims for damage.

A CIP catalogue record for this title is available from the British Library.

ISBN: 978-1-80074-304-5

The opinions expressed in this book are the author's own and do not reflect the views of the publisher, author's employer, organization, committee or other group or individual

First Published in 2022

Olympia Publishers
Tallis House
2 Tallis Street
London
EC4Y 0AB

Printed in Great Britain

Dedication

To, You

Acknowledgements

I would like to acknowledge my mother for keeping my head above water.

Die for a day

I wish…
I wish I could die
Just for a day
Just one day
So I could see your face when you are told the news
So that I can feel the lump rise in your throat
So that I can be the metaphoric truck that hits you
Knocking you off balance as you fall to the floor
Grasping for anything that feels like me.

You taught me

You taught me to love country music
Which my brothers hate.
You taught me to crack my knuckles
Which my mother hates.

A gray dream

In my dream last night I asked you,
"Do you love her?"
You replied
"No you were my light. She is gray"
I woke up smiling because you said exactly what I wanted to hear
If you asked me I would tell you I didn't love any of the men that came after you either
The smile quickly faded
It wasn't really *you* that said it
It was the subconscious part of my mind
The part that tells me what I want so desperately to hear.

Uncomfortable love

I'm not questioning whether or not you still love me
I know you probably do
Even if it's just a little it's still there
I'm still existing in your heart
What I don't understand
What I do question is
What are you doing about it?
Nothing
You are doing nothing with the love you may still hold for me
Or are you mixing it up with the love you've developed for her?
Are you giving her the love that belongs to me?
Left over from after me and before her.
Mixing it
Kneading it like dough until it takes the shape of just one love
In a way
It's comforting that it's existing in someone's heart
Not just floating aimlessly stuck between the space of you and me
But it doesn't belong to her
It's mine
It will never fit quite right in her
It will feel like an uncomfortable love
You will forever be in uncomfortable love.

The first apology

Let me apologize to you
I want to tell you how sorry I am
I'm sorry that you wanted to fix her
You didn't deserve that responsibility
I'm sorry that I put you in a position you weren't
equipped to be in
I'm sorry that now all your demons look a little bit like her
And I'm sorry that I can't take that away
I'm sorry that in the end
You didn't just lose me
You lost your best friend

After you

There is an after you
And I'm waiting for my heart to hear those words before my mind for once
Here is what I know
I loved you…
No
I love you
Present tense
To this day
I love you
But I don't wish you could hear me when I say it to the wind anymore
You never heard me say it face to face with nothing between us but empty air
Where my I love you would land
Somewhere between us where are the promises, secrets that were never told
And where your I love you landed
Never quite reaching me
I heard you say it
Three times that night before I said it back
So here is what I know
I loved you back all three times
I will love you back every day after you.

Ego

You walk on your tiptoes
And the only reason I can think of
Is that you're trying to reach your ego
Keep tipping
You might reach it one day.

She is beautiful

You are in everyone I see
I hear your laugh and my heart does a backflip
I see your smile flashed by on a stranger
And every nerve ending in my body jolts awake
Sending me spiraling through the air
Trying to push me back in time
To the first time I made you laugh
It's never quite right though
There's always something missing
And that of course is you
The fundamental part of you that makes you who you are
And it makes me wonder
Is it still a part of you?
Or did you give it to me the day you left?
Because you knew I would need it to keep me
From being completely without you
Because being completely without you
Would hurt like complete hell
But this
This gift of the little parts of you that I carry
Might just hurt worse than hell
It's purgatory
Stuck in the middle between heaven and hell
It doesn't lean closer to one side or the other
I still smile
But it's empty
I still laugh
But there's a void between breaths

My eyes that you said you loved so much
No longer dance with excitement
Do you remember?
Please tell me you remember
Or is there not room left in your heart to remember
things about me
Because she has it now
And she is beautiful

.

.

.

I hear your laugh
And my heart somersaults down to the bottom of my
stomach
I see your smile flash by on a stranger's face
And every nerve ending in my body implodes
And if you gave it to me as a goodbye gift I don't want it
So please
Take it back
Give it to her because
She
Is beautiful.

Kisses soaked in alcohol

My favorite times are the nights we spend together
Talking, laughing, getting drunk off our kisses soaked in alcohol
You taste like Coors Light and the chew tobacco you promised your mother you had quit
I will never stop loving it
It's become muscle memory
Did I mention that I love you?
When we go to sleep together
In your bed that's even too small for one person
We sleep back-to-back
We don't need to face each other to prove our love can withstand the night
We are real
I fall asleep to the rhythm of your breathing
You're so soothing to my racing mind
And right as I'm drifting off you whisper
I love you into the air
And I float on top of the words all night.
My favorite times are the days we spend together
One hour spilling into another
Until it turns into another night spent together
Kisses soaked in alcohol
Did I mention that I love you?
It was the night we spent
Watching the weirdest movie we could find
Taking a drink every time we were confused by it
I've never been more drunk

And you've never loved me more
In that moment between laughter and a few drunk kisses
I felt it
You are my forever
Did I mention that I love you?

OK

We promised never to say it to each other
And we never did
Unless we were really upset at the other
Saying okay was fine
As long as it was
O-K-A-Y
But O-K
That was the saddest word I knew
I felt like saying OK was like saying the love had run out
And that day that's exactly what it meant
Our last words to each other
"So I guess it's over now we're really done"
"OK"
I don't even remember who said it
All I remember was the air getting sucked out of the room
And I felt like I might actually die
After everything
After I gave you every part of me
My body
My mind
My heart
Every part of who I was anymore
Was tied together with you
What did you give me that wasn't immediately taken away when you left?
Nothing
There was nothing left
There was no need for me to tell you how badly you had

just broken me
All that was left
Was OK.

Empty swing

There's a swing on the front porch of my house
It's where I sat all summer waiting for you
Waiting for a text
Waiting for a phone call
Waiting for you to pick me up
It's where I sat in the middle of the night when anxiety would overtake me
Every day and almost every night
I sat there waiting for something
Cut to Act One of my perfect world
I come home from a day that almost broke me
Which happens a lot
But you would be sitting there on that swing waiting for me
I sit down next to you and rest my head on your shoulder
And we sit there
Together
All night
And it doesn't even matter what we would talk about
Because you simply showed up
And that's all I really needed
For you to just show up
Cut to Act Two of my reality
I'm standing in my kitchen watching the blood drip down my arm
You promised that you would spend the night with me
And after only two hours
You had to go home

Something your mom needed your help with.
I knew it was a lie by the way you looked away every time
I tried to meet your eyes
So you left
And I thought about that porch swing
And how it was empty
And how you were never going to sit with me on it
And in that moment
I snapped
I started in the bathroom but the razor was too dull
The kitchen was next
I found the biggest knife
And I cut a line in my arm for every lie you told me that day
Then out of nowhere you call me
I'm reluctant but I answer on the last ring
I snapped out of whatever trance I was in
I look down and there is blood all over the floor and sink
And the knife
I'm still holding the knife.
Cut to Act Three of my reality
I'm in the hospital and the nurse is trying to bandage up my arm
While the doctor talks to my parents in the hall
I don't want to hear what they're saying
So I focus on the door
Waiting for it to open
For you to come in and sit next to me
But you don't
Cut to Act Four of my reality
You knew what happened

You knew I was too dangerous to be left alone
But you didn't turn your car around
And the next day you didn't call
And the day after that
The porch swing was still empty.

Psychic

The psychic told me that you and I would last
But not forever
She said we would be great friends
And we were
You were my favorite person
But like she said
It didn't last forever.

Losing my mind

One day my mother asked me if I had lost my mind
And before I could scream YES PLEASE HELP ME!
I whispered no
I'm fine
That night I slept on the floor because my bed felt too soft
That's the thing about mental illness
No one notices something is wrong
Until you're so far gone
That turning around feels like it might kill you before you kill yourself
Staying alive isn't the easy way out
I started cutting on my thigh so no one could see it
But summer quickly came
And so did a day I felt okay for the first time in awhile
That day I went to the pool with a friend
And I almost forgot about the cuts and scars
Until I saw it on her face
She saw them
And neither one of us said anything
The moment stuck in the air like glue
And I sank even farther into myself.

Another after

After you is a puffy face from crying myself to sleep
After you is silence in the car
Driving with no music
After you is gaining sixty pounds
Because eating was the only thing that didn't hurt
After you is not being able to drink my favorite coffee
Because it tastes like our morning kisses
After you is slowly forgetting the sound of your voice
After you is not laughing at anything
Because nothing is funny anymore
After you is sex with a stranger
But after me?
After me is an empty passenger seat
After me is going out every night trying to drown the memory of us
After me is no more middle of the day "thinking about you" texts
After me is never hearing my voice telling you that I love you forever
After me is no thigh to grab while you're driving
After us everything feels like the earth tilted
And the ground will never settle beneath our feet
Because I still believe
There never should have been an after.

Gun to my head

I'll never be the same
There are days I look back and wish I had seen you coming
I could have dodged the bullet
But if I'm being honest with myself
I would stand in front of the gun
Watching you pull the trigger
Time and time again.

But don't you love me?

Two days after we broke up you agreed to come talk to me
We sat in the car and I listened as you apologized for not turning around
When I needed you most
But I already forgave you
Two minutes after it happened
Because that's what you do when you love someone
You forgive them
I was sobbing that uncontrollable ugly cry
A few tears streamed down your face
And I asked you
"But don't you love me?"
As if loving me made up for anything
To me it did
Even though you broke me like I didn't even matter that day
I wanted it all back
And I would have sat in your car
Until there was nothing left to say but "Yes, let's try again."
And that's exactly what we said.

Break

Everything I could say to you sounds so trivial
Against the way you made me feel
You didn't just break my heart
You broke who I was.

Mania in the eyes

At 9:07 a.m. I text my mom
"I feel great today, I even put on earrings."
By 7:36 p.m. my ears hurt from the earrings
And my head is in the toilet as I throw up what's left of a panic attack
I'm afraid of the mornings that I feel great
It's been just three years since I was told by a stranger
With four degrees framed on the wall behind her
That these "great mornings" are a manic state
And every manic morning ends in a crashing night
Hence the head in the toilet
But no matter how many manic mornings I have
The crashing nights always catch me off guard
There are times that the mania lasts for days
I'm in such a good mood
And I can go for hours
Nonstop
Without feeling the least bit tired
But there's always a moment I catch my reflection
And my wild eyes scare me
And I think to myself
Something is wrong
I mean nothing is wrong
I mean everything is wrong
No
Something is definitely wrong
But who cares? I feel great!
Until it happens

And I don't feel great anymore
The crash
And it's so strong it physically hurts to move
I get a glimpse of my reflection and this time
My dead eyes scare me
And I whisper to myself
I can't do this anymore.

Do you?

Every day that passes
I get further away from you
And I don't think I'd recognize who you are now
Because all of the things you were with me
Are probably gone now
Do you have the same favorite color?
It was purple just like mine
Do you still only get cheese on your pizza?
That used to drive me nuts
Do you still love the same crappy football team?
I don't actually know if they're crappy I just know they lost a lot
Do you still drink too much?
Do you still carry the weight of whatever it was
That tormented you every day?
Three years and two cities between us
And I don't know who you've become
And I'll probably never know
So I'll keep feeling you forget me
While I forget you
More and more every day.

11:11

I didn't just lose you as a lover
I lost you as a best friend
You were my favorite person
And I think that's why it hurts so badly
And I am so angry with you
I hate you
I hate you
I…
Don't hate you
And that makes me hate you
It wasn't just my heart you broke
You broke who I was
And every day you break who I am
And I know I shouldn't give you that much power
How I feel now after you is my fault
I've been through enough therapy to know that
I'm struggling to forgive you
Because I just don't know how
Every day it hurts a little less
Until I flash back to a memory
A memory of secret winks we would exchange in crowds of people
And I can still feel that first initial blow to my heart
And it hurts
It hurts so bad
Every prayer
Shooting star
Birthday

Clock striking 11:11 wish is always the same
"Make the pain stop please"
I am convinced that one day
Your smile
And the freckles on your nose
Will all just be features on a face I used to know
At least I can continue to wish for
Every prayer
To just be a prayer
Every shooting star
To just be a star
Every birthday
Just a birthday
And one day when the clock hits 11:11
It will just be the time of day.

I promise to stay alive

There were four guys after you
And maybe if I kept my eyes closed
I could have loved them
I was trying so hard to replace you
One had your eyes
Almost
One had your laugh
Almost
One smelled like you
Almost
The last was the exact opposite of you
None of them were what I needed to get over you
I wasn't replacing you
I was begging the universe to send you back to me
Even if it was you in a different person
I would be able to find you in him
Pick out the parts that reminded me most of you
I could recreate you in someone
Who wanted me as much as I wanted you
But that's never going to happen
And now I don't speak to any of them
Just like I don't speak to you
I am alone
I am lonely
And nothing's funny anymore
I want to promise myself that when I meet the next guy
I won't pick him to pieces trying to find you
Because you are gone

I don't want to find that I've lost all of it
But I don't know if I was ever who you needed
And that kills me because I would have given you everything
One night we got drunk and for a minute my tongue was sober
And I said to you
"I won't die for you, but I will stay alive for you"
I think you thought I was telling a stupid joke
But I wasn't
Staying alive was all I had left
And I was giving it to you.

Shame

You made me blame my mental illness for all of our problems
When I was manic
I was out of control too much to deal with
When I sunk into my depression
Each time further than the last
You would tell me you couldn't save me
I wasn't waiting for you to save me
I was waiting for you to tell me
I was strong enough to save myself
And that you'd stay next to me while I picked up each piece
One at a time
That night I called you when panic was drowning me
And you sent me to voicemail followed with a text
"I'm having dinner with my parents, what do you need?"
I needed you
In that moment I had no one
And after I read that text I knew I was alone
I came out of that panic attack more broken than when I went into it
And from that night forward with each attack
I felt shame
I was ashamed of who this mental illness was turning me into
Fast forward three years and the shame is beginning to shed from my skin
I have an illness

But that's not who I am
And now I see you are the one who should feel ashamed
You turned your back
You did that
And I'm not saying I'm an innocent victim in this
Because I'm not
I threw it all in your face with pleading hands
Begging for help
You didn't deserve that
I put shame on myself
You just didn't stop me.

Heart

We were surrounded by dying flowers and wilting balloons
It was two days after Valentine's Day in the grocery store where we worked
You were in a depleting relationship and I was in love with you
As we were laughing and popping balloons
You picked up a plastic red heart and handed it to me
I kept it in the pocket of my apron for close to a year
A year goes by so quickly when all you want is for time to stand still
That's a moment I wish I could stay in for just a minute longer
Because even though you weren't mine
That pocket-sized heart meant that we did exist
That we were real
Even just for a moment.

Monday–Thursday Friday–Sunday

Every week was the same
Monday through Thursday texting all day
Talking about how much we missed each other
Friday through Sunday I was begging you to drive an hour to see me
An hour should feel like nothing to drive when you really want to see someone
But you didn't really want to see me did you?
You kept me on the hook all week
Promising me that one day things would be better
That we'd only have to say goodnight not goodbye
I revolved my whole existence around when you might want to see me
And when you did come
It would only be for as long as a movie and a kiss goodbye
Every time you left a part of me got chipped away
I was becoming a shell of a person
While you stayed whole
To this day I don't know how I survived you
And I know this all seems so trivial
That I sound crazy for loving you that much
When all the signs to walk away were there
Right in my face
But I latched onto you when I was far away from myself
And I couldn't
I could not let you go
Even if all we were was a movie and a kiss goodbye.

Where is my God?

Dear God
I believe in you
But I don't feel you
My mother and brother have such a strong faith.
So why am I here feeling so empty?
Where were you when my world was turning upside down?
When I would pray so hard for some sense of relief from my own mind
You didn't ease it
If your hands create everything
Why did you build my brain to hate itself?
You breathed life into my lungs
But allowed me to want so badly to end it
When I woke up in that hospital room
Where the bed was bolted to the floor
With bars on the windows
I did not feel you with me
I felt fear
Fear of myself
Fear of the world that you created
When they cleaned and rewrapped the bandage on my arm
I did not feel you with me
Instead I felt the sting of the wound cleaner
Seeping into the cuts on my arm
When I cried myself to sleep every night I was there
I did not feel you with me
I've never felt more alone

That New Year's Eve night
When I found myself in the apartment of a boy I hardly knew
When the weight of his body was on top of me
And his teeth were biting and splitting open my lip
While I struggled to get away
I did not feel you with me
When I fell so deeply in love with someone that was always going to break me
I did not feel you with me
Ever since I was a little girl
I was told that you were with us
Through our brightest and darkest times
So maybe I've been wrong all along
And the further I get away from that year
The clearer I see it
Maybe you have always been there
And maybe the proof is as simple as that
I'm still here
Maybe that's all the proof I need
Yesterday was a beautiful day
And as I was driving I started singing along to the radio
And I felt happy for the first time in over a year
And I realized that if that year had never happened
I would never know how precious that moment in the car was
I can still feel the ache of that time to my very core
And that's just it I get to feel it. It's you.

Reflection

I built us up so high
And it was a long way down when we fell
And I don't know how much I'll have to write
Until I can explain how fiercely you broke me
And I don't know how many times I have to write that you're gone
Before it finally sinks in
Three or thirty years away from you
I don't know if it's ever going to feel real
I have tried to
Talk
Scream
Cry
And write you out of existence
And I'm still yearning every day for answers to the same questions
Over and over again
Maybe my answer is that there is no answer
That the way you treated me has nothing to do with me at all
The way you treated me is a reflection of the way you feel about yourself
And that makes me feel sorry for you
Because there must be a huge void where your heart should be.

The competition is not real

I was always competing with someone or something
Something that didn't even exist
Competing against your ex-girlfriend you still wanted
Competing against your friends
Because you always wanted to spend more time with them than me
Trying to keep up with your drinking
Even when it would make me physically sick
You never made me feel like I was enough for you
I tried everything I could think of to keep you interested
And in the end all that work I put into us was a waste
I couldn't be your ex-girlfriend
Because I was me
I was never going to fit in with your friends
Because I was me
And I would never be able to drink like you
Because I was me
And that should have been enough.

Another apology

Once
I broke a boy's heart
I watched it break behind his eyes
I immediately wanted to take it back
Tell him I didn't know what I was saying
But I didn't
I heard myself tell him I didn't love him
Not the way he wanted to love me
I watched myself move as far away from him in his car as
I could
And I stared out the window
I felt myself hate myself just a little bit more
I want to tell you how sorry I am
For thinking I was in love with him
And that I could or would never love you
I should have let him go
Because he was never going to be good for me
And when he broke me like you warned me he would
I still wouldn't admit that you were right
That summer day we spent hiking through the state park
It felt like we were the only two people in the world
We talked the whole time about anything and everything
It always felt like we had known each other for years
I didn't feel like that with him
Not once
I want to tell you how sorry I am
And how if I could go back and make a better decision
I would in a second

Because I know you would have loved me
Exactly the way I needed to be loved at that time
You never cared that I had bipolar
And you never held my bad days against me
I was never ashamed of my mind with you
All of the midnight car rides
That I took for granted
I will never get back
And I'm so happy that you found someone
That knows how to appreciate and love you
She's so lucky to have you
I know I was
I know that now

Tall, brown hair and beautiful

Immediately after we ended I wanted to replace you
And that's exactly what I set out to do
And then there he was
Tall, brown hair, and beautiful
So I gave him my number
And when he texted me
I knew I was going to replace you
Well I was going to try my best
It was my twenty first birthday and he wanted to take me out
Little did I know that him taking me out meant a sports bar
Where I had one drink
When we left he wanted to drive around so we did
And when we parked in the middle of nowhere
I knew I was either about to be murdered
Or kissed
I was kissed
And then kissed again
And then he was trying to go too far
I stopped him and he took me home
It was such a long awkward drive
And then it was over
And I went to my room
Sat on my bed
Looked in the mirror
And the red lipstick suddenly looked stupid on me
Like I was trying too hard

I sat there
And sat there
And sat there
Until I almost convinced myself that I had a good time
And I repeated this two more times
Go on the mediocre date
Push him off me after the second kiss
Regret the red lipstick
Until he asked me to go to his house
Which I agreed to… stupid
I tried to talk to him about my struggle with mental illness
He didn't hear me
Or he didn't care
Or both
So I gave him what he wanted
So maybe he would see me
When it was over so were we
My chances of replacing you were back to zero
Along with the chances he'd ever call me again
And I should have been very upset
I don't know if I was so broken over you
That I couldn't possibly feel hurt by anyone else
Or if I just didn't care enough about myself to care
I think I got my answer on the drive home
When I drove in silence for a few miles and then realized
I don't remember this guy's last name.

I want that love

I want to know what being in love feels like
True love
You know the kind of love
Where both people feel the exact same way about each other
I know it exists because I've seen it
I've seen it with my brother and his girlfriend
I've seen it with older couples I've taken care of
Movies
Books
Reality television
It's out there and I want to know it
Some days I have pure honest hope that it will happen for me
But most days I'm so down on myself that I wonder
How is anyone going to love me
When loving myself seems like such an impossible task
But I still want to love with the innocence of a child
Like I've never felt the sting of a heartbreak
Like life hasn't beaten me down more times than it's lifted me up
Like I'm still whole
I've sampled bitter
And it's only left me with a bad taste in my mouth
So I will actively choose to think every day
That one day
Someone will look at me with such tenderness
That I might actually recognize
And I'll think to myself
There you are.

Our future lives in the past

I can't believe I got this far
We went from two strangers innocently flirting
To staying up late talking about what we're going to name our dog
That we would get when we moved in together
Today when I think about our whole story
My heart sinks into my stomach
And my hands shake
Some days it's sadness
Some days it's anger
Most days it's nostalgia
I haven't cried over you in awhile
But I have been angry with you for a few months now
And I'm not sure if
Sadness
Anger
Or nostalgia
Hurts the most.

Demons

Sometimes I wonder what would have happened
If I was successful in killing myself
Would you have turned around then?
Or just leave me for dead
I was so caught up in your demons
That I couldn't see my own taking over my mind
Waiting for just the right moment
And then
Boom
The moment of impact
So strong it knocked me out of my mind and took over
I was on autopilot
Going through the motions
With one thing flashing in my mind
Like a neon sign in one of those bars you escape to
"You have to make it stop"
So I hurt myself
And while I was hurting myself you were driving away
With no remorse or sense of empathy
What if you had seen the blood?
Would it splatter itself in your dreams every night?
I wouldn't really hope that for you
But I do wish I could make you never forget
I hope that on a Tuesday morning
When you're getting ready for work
And you go to kiss her goodbye
A drop of blood drips out of your nose
And lands on your brand new white carpet

You both look down
And she blames it on how dry the air is in the house
during the winter
You go along with it
But you know it's your demon
The one you can't get away from
No matter how successful you are at work
No matter who you marry
No matter where you go
Or who you fuck
That demon will always be there
With eyes like mine
And while you're being tortured
I will go on with my life
As if I didn't almost let you ruin it
You won't feel it every day
Sometimes you'll go so long without feeling it
That you'll forget that it exists
But it will always come back
I survived you
I wonder
Can you survive me?

Existence

No matter how hard I try
I cannot write you out of existence
And I try every day
But you're still in this world
Living your life
As if nothing happened between us
Like you didn't kiss me in the cooler at work
Just because you said you wanted to see me smile
I still think you wanted to taste my smile
And by the way your lips mirrored mine
As they curved up into a smile
I could tell you liked the way it tasted
How do you kiss her every day
And not flash back to me?
Maybe I didn't have as much of an effect on you
As I hoped I did
Maybe that kiss
Was just a kiss
You are the bad guy in all of my stories
Only at the end though
In the beginning you save me from myself
Yes you kissed me at work
But in the dark
Cold
Empty cooler
Where no one could see us
Once
You refused to kiss me in the parking lot after dinner

Because there were too many people around
Strangers
These people were strangers
And you were too embarrassed to kiss me in front of them
Take a moment to think about that
How humiliating that was
In that story you were the bad guy
That time you called me drunk
You told me you loved me
The next day you texted me
And said you didn't mean it
That it was a joke
That's a pretty twisted joke
I am not where you left me
I am in a much better place
I got a job
A car
I'm on the right medication
I feel like a different person
My hair is longer
And I've gained some weight
I look like a different person
I wonder if I met you now
Would I even like you?

Apology to a nineteen-year-old girl

Today I am sorry
And for once I'm not sorry to him
I'm sorry to the girl I was
For wanting more than anything to be wanted
I wish you could feel how young nineteen really is
Too young to make someone your everything
Too young to know what you wanted
Compared to what you needed
But he made you laugh
That is not enough
He thought you were beautiful
That is not enough
He said he loved you
That is still not enough
He blamed you for all that was wrong with your relationship
Your immaturity
Emotions
And mostly your mental illness
Were not to blame
His unwillingness to meet you where you were
And the way he knew he was never going to fully love you
The way you needed to be loved
Is what was to blame
I know how alone you felt
At the time your parents were going through a tough divorce
And you had just been diagnosed bipolar
That's a lot to take in

For anyone
He was the only person you physically saw every day
He was your constant
But that didn't mean he was right for you
I wish I could go back and shake you
Until your mind straightened out
So that you can see he was only in love with the chase
Not you
I'm sorry that you gave him everything
Your mind
Your heart
And I'm sorry he took your body and made it his own
And I'm sorry that it makes you feel dirty
I'm sorry that sometimes thinking about it all at once makes you sick
You wanted him so badly it actually hurt
But you do not need him
All you need is yourself
If I could go back
I would dry every tear
And put back every piece he broke
I'm sorry it feels like he stole something from you
And I'm sorry that he did take a part of you
But it's a part you don't want
Desperation
I wish I could tell you that you're going to meet someone
Who won't want anything but love from you
But I don't know that
At least not yet
Don't get bitter
That's not who you are
It's going to take time to learn to be thankful to him

For making you laugh when you were so sad
But time takes time
You can go through it all
Every conversation
Text
Phone call
Argument
Make up
And break up
It will never make sense why he hurt you in such a deep way
You have to get to the point where it doesn't matter "why"
All that matters is how you choose to accept it
And you have to learn to accept it.
So he made you laugh
That's not enough
So he thought you were beautiful
That's not enough
So he loved you
That is still not enough
But you are enough
You always have been
And it will get easier
Every day
Even when you don't want it to
Because staying stuck in it is sometimes easier
But you are going to get better
One day you'll catch yourself not thinking about him
And you'll feel it
All you ever needed
Was you.

Midnight thoughts

When I met you
I was already apologizing
For who I was.

Stay stuck

Throughout my years in school
Pre-K to high school
I always felt alone in the crowded hallways
So when I turned eighteen my senior year
I'd sign myself out of school almost every day
I'd tell my mom I had
A stomach ache
Sore throat
Headache
Cramps
Once I even told her I sneezed
You know wouldn't want to catch a cold
I know she knew I was lying
But she knew something was wrong with me
And she was lost in her own life
Getting divorced after twenty-four years of marriage does something to a person
Even under the best circumstances
So I would go to school every morning and leave
Sometimes before the first bell even rang
I didn't know I was fighting a mental illness
I thought I just couldn't get my shit together
Because it seemed like it was so easy to everyone else
I wasn't one of those super smart kids
That could skip school and still pass all my classes
I failed
Almost every class
Both semesters

So I didn't graduate
And I was full of so much shame but at the same time
Relief
School was over and I thought
So were the days of feeling alone
But the lonely didn't go away
It grew to half my size
And stuck itself to my back
It was like carrying a book bag I could never take off
Since then it hasn't shrunk
Or gotten bigger
It just sits there
And it makes me wonder
Did it stick itself to me
Or did I stick myself to it?

Connections

There are two girls in this world that I am connected to
And they don't even know I exist
Because you keep me a secret
One is a girl you dated three years before me
You used to tell me that she and I were complete opposites
You said she was exactly your type
So why did you even want me?
She broke up with you
And it slit your ego in half
I know because I watched you turn into a huge
Well for lack of a better word
Asshole
You wanted her back
Don't think I didn't notice
The disappointment in your voice when you answered the phone that night
And it wasn't her on the other end
Instead it was me
The second is a girl you are with now after me
Who looks just like the first girl but with longer hair
She is the one you were looking for
The whole time you were with me
And you post pictures of the two of you together
All the time
Very much unlike you when you were with me
And you wouldn't take pictures with me
Let alone post them

For people to see that we were together
And yes it still bothers me to see it
I don't know anything about her
Other than she's definitely your type
The opposite of me
All three of us have kissed you
We have all heard you say I love you
We have all seen you
Happy
Sad
Angry
And everything in between
You have told each of us that we were forever
You have planned futures with each of us
And lied to at least two of us about these futures
But I was the one that was a secret
You hid me
Lied to me
Humiliated me
And for what?
What makes me not as special as the other two?
What makes me not good enough for you?
Wait
Let me change my train of thought real quick…
Why weren't you man enough to come forward
And claim me as yours?
Because I am just as special as the other two
And despite your best efforts
You didn't permanently break me
There are two girls in this world that I am connected to
And they don't even know I exist

And as I write this today
I am not embarrassed of that thought
Because even though that says
That you have put shame on
Who I was and what we were
I am giving the shame back to myself
And throwing it all on you.

Here's some advice

I'm going to take a minute to talk to you
The reader
I want to give you some tips
That I wish someone had told me.

- Take your medication, the prescribed dose every day even when you feel like you don't need it
- Don't fight the panic attacks, just let them happen even if you're in public. Go somewhere quiet, sit down, put your head in your hands and count until your breathing settles
- Don't hate yourself for having a mental illness. Whatever you have, it's not your fault
- Don't stop praying, even when God is the last person you want to talk to
- Pet your dog
- Laugh when something is funny
- Cry when you need to, even if it's the third time that day
- Paint your nails a color other than black for a week
- Sing whenever you can, even if it's awful
- Try not to drink every night
- Forgive your parents for not being perfect
- Buy the dress
- Eat the cake
- Love like you've never felt the sting of rejection, but don't forget you have
- Sleep in
- Kiss whoever you want, whenever you want

- Hug your mother
- Don't forget to live while you're just trying to survive
- Listen to everything around you. People, traffic, music, birds
- Spend too much time in the candle aisle smelling them all
- Eat too much with your best friend
- Clean your room
- Shave your legs
- Take a picture of the pretty sky, even if that's all you have in your camera roll
- Love your own smile as much as you love your favorite person's
- Watch your favorite movie for the tenth time
- Be proud of every day you're alive
- It won't feel like it for a long time, but you will get over him. Even if it's an inch at a time. This pain can't last forever. It won't last forever
I promise.

Cover to cover

The therapist gave me a notebook in the hospital
She told me to write in it every day
At least a few sentences about how I was feeling day to day
I filled it with thoughts of you
Even though I was in a psychiatric hospital
After trying to kill myself
Still my only thoughts were about you
And I thought that was love
I thought that we were love
I want to make something clear
Surrendering all of who you are
And replacing it with all that he is
Is not love
You won't have to surrender any part of yourself for love
I filled that notebook
Cover to cover with our story
While I was writing it, it felt like a love story
But reading it today
It just made me sad for that girl
She wasn't even the main character of her own story
I thought about getting rid of the notebook
Ripping it up
Throwing it in the trash
Burning it
Burying it six feet under ground
Like the casket of someone I didn't even love
Instead I put it on the bottom shelf of my nightstand

Like the bad hiding spot of a child
Still in sight but not too obvious at first glance
I am not ashamed of it at all
I am proud of it
I lived it
Page by page.

Three years until I'm my own

Even if the world didn't want you
I still did
I wish you could feel the life you took out of me
While I was trying to love you
But you never will
They say karma is real
And if it is
That means you will fall so far in love with someone
That you won't feel like you can function without
But if karma is real
She won't love you the same way
And you'll have to live in that agony you caused me
I'm just trying to remember what it feels like to have a heartbeat
One that doesn't beat to bring life to you
The emptiness that brought me was so heavy
I dressed for you
I undressed for you
The only time I felt like I had you to myself
And I'd like to have myself back
I want my body back
Before you ever saw or touched it
I should have held onto it
Kept it to myself
You weren't the first boy to have my body
And you won't be the last
But you were the only one that I felt like I lost my innocence with

I read somewhere that every seven years
Every cell in your body is destroyed
And replaced
That means in four years I'll have a body that you have never touched
I can finally say I want a life that you're not in
A body you've never touched
I am part of a world that doesn't want you and I together
And for the first time in years
I am relieved.

Borrowed strength

The psychic said that you and I wouldn't last
Her exact words were
"You will be best friends for a while   but he is not the one."
I wanted more than anything for her to be wrong
When I went to see her again she was gone
It felt like she dropped a ticking time bomb in my hands
And I couldn't put it down
Like it was meant to blow up in my face
And it did
I took the blunt of the explosion
But the shrapnel hit everyone around me
My best friend felt it when I didn't want to hang out anymore
My brothers felt it when I stopped joking with them
My mother felt it every time she looked into my eyes and it wasn't me behind them anymore
My coworkers felt it when I quit my job
It flew through two cities
And hit you when you woke up alone in bed that morning
I'm not the only heart you broke
There's no going back after this
And so I am left
Mending my own wounds
And the wounds of everyone around me
That psychic saw something in you through me
And it wasn't something good
When we finally broke up for good

I don't know where the strength to walk away came from
I know it had to come from somewhere or someone else
Because I know it didn't come from me
I wasn't that strong then
I like to think that it was her
The psychic
That she planted something in my mind
Something that told me walking away was the only option
I know it was borrowed strength
I know that whatever strength it was
I still have a part of it
And that is so comforting.

Blake

My mind keeps flashing back to that summer night you took me to the fair
After he broke up with me
The first time
I wanted to be there with you
But my mind was with him
We ran into three friends that night
Each asked where he was and why we were there together
Before you could speak I said
You and I were just friends
And things with him and I were complicated
I know now how cruel that was of me to say
Especially when I knew how you felt about me
And that you just wanted me to have a good time
And be happy with you
When we got on that ride together I blurted out
That him and I were going to talk and work things out
I saw the blood rush out of your face
And in that moment I knew I was hurting you
But I didn't stop
I just kept talking about how I missed him
On and on
Until even I wanted to tell myself to shut the hell up
When you took me home it was silent in the car
But the tension was deafening
I knew I just ruined any chance I would ever have with you
I want to tell you that you are the only man I've had in my

life
That stands out as a real man
I want to thank you for every time you held my hand
I felt safe with you
And I've never had that before
I've written this apology four different times
But the words just feel flat compared to how sorry I really am
My hope is that one day I'll have the chance to apologize
In person
So that you can see it on my face that this isn't an empty apology
I mean it with everything in me
I hurt you and I knew I was doing it
And that act is unforgivable
I mostly want to thank you for your friendship
You never had any hidden agendas with me
You just wanted me to be happy
That's it
And happiness is what I needed most at the time
And I threw it away like it was nothing
I wish I knew then that it was everything
You are a great person
You're kind
Loving
Smart
You have integrity
You're soft where the world is hard
And you never falter on who you are
I really admire you
I remember that Valentine's Day you sent me flowers

They came in this mug with hearts all over it
I still have that mug
And I drink tea out of it when I'm having a bad day
It still makes me smile
Even though there's a crack in it
That's pretty ironic when you think about it
I know you found someone else and you've moved on with your life
And when I see you together
I can see that she really does love you
That makes me so happy for you
Because you really deserve that
For what it's worth
I wish you the absolute best
Even if it's without me.

Pocket size

I thought I found God in your laughter
But it was only a boy
Not yet a man
And not close to becoming one
I put you on such a high pedestal
So high you could have reached up and touched the sky while sitting down
But you were too small
And the edges too jagged to fit into the space I built for you
Your love was the same way
Too small for the space I needed it to fill
And like a stone I kept it in my pocket
Where I thought it was safe
Safe from the world's judgment
Safe from losing it
And safe from you trying to take it away
Throwing it out the window onto a gravel road
Where I'd never find it again
Eleven months later when our love was put to the test
I reached in my pocket to feel what was left
I pulled out a pebble
I held it in the palm of my hand
And with the same breath you used to say your last words to me
It blew away in the wind
And your love for me was gone
Just like that
A pocket-sized love
That never had a chance of surviving.

Thank you

"Let's stay friends"
The unofficial, official line said in a break up
But you never even offered that
We were over
That was it
You were completely done with me
I wasn't ready to not have you in my life
And sometimes I don't know if I want this book to end
Because the moment I write the last letter of the last word on the last page
I will have written our time out this present world of existence
All the words I have ever wanted to say about you
To you
Will only exist on these pages
And I'm going to begin a whole new part of my life
That you won't know me in
Sometimes I wish you could see just how far I've come
Away from that broken girl that you ended things with that December morning
The girl you decided wasn't even worth the lie of
"Let's stay friends"
I want to thank you for being my rock bottom
Because I shaped myself into someone that can live without you
Someone I'm happy exists
If I had stayed with you
I would have died

At the fault of my own hands
With your lies and misleadings as weapons
So in a way you saved my life
By ending ours together
So thank you

Snow falls in April

The feeling of being with you
Was like the first time it snows in April
After a full week of weather mimicking summer days
That moment when the gray sky releases the cold flakes it's been holding in
Hiding behind white clouds
You see we were nothing but an illusion of a good thing
It masked itself
Over a stupid fight
Or a night crying myself to sleep
We were always one lie away from the temperature of the room dropping
The sky opening up and letting something cold and silent fall over us
Yesterday when it snowed for the first time in April
It brought me to you in my mind
And I couldn't breathe
But the snow only covered the ground in patches
And by the time the sun made it to the middle of the sky
It was gone
And when there was no evidence of it even happening
I came back to myself
And the puddles on the sidewalk were only puddles
Not a metaphor of our love melting into nothing
The cold nip in the air didn't want me to hold onto you for warmth
Instead I zipped up my own jacket
And put my hands in my own pockets

I kept myself warm
And by next spring
When the sky has to release one last snow fall
I will not fight all the metaphors I can come up with
Instead I will name then all
One by one
Until
I can exhale

A moment of impact

The moment of impact
When my father's fist put a hole in the wall in the hallway
on the day of his mother's funeral
Drywall falling to the ground
The moment you kissed me in the cooler at work
The smell of fresh produce surrounding us
The first time I took a pair of scissors to my arm
I remember the blood but I don't feel the pain
Moments that play out in slow motion in your mind
When you think back to them
I can remember you in pieces
Your smile always comes first
But then fades
And your eyes flash through my memory
But I cannot envision your whole face in my mind at once
I think a lot about moments of impact
And why certain times are faded
While others you feel happening like you're reliving the moment
The farther away from us I get the less I can relive
And I wonder how long it's going to be
Until I can't relive us anymore
The moment of the night I took my first pill
One to ease the noise in my head
I felt it slowly calming me
Until there was no more noise
I see the orange pill bottles on the windowsill
And they are a constant reminder

That I am only okay one pill at a time
That I could forget to take a pill
And be only a moment away from crashing back down
Into the nothing I became with you
The moments I wish to relive are slowly becoming less about you
And more about beautiful moments I created myself
Without you
There are times when I want to be not okay for awhile
When the exhaustion of trying to hold myself together for so long takes over
And I can't physically do it anymore
Those are the times I stop taking care of myself
Where I won't shower
Because the thought of the water touching my skin makes me want to cry
Or when washing my hair feels like an impossible task
But those feelings don't last forever
They never do
Because they are moments
And moments pass
Time goes by and my father fixes the hole in the wall
Covering a painful memory
I walk through the produce section in the store
But it doesn't hurt anymore
It just feels like the last innocent memory
Before our painful story began
There are three scars on my left arm from the scissors
But now they are covered by a tattoo that says
"Let's leave the weeping to the willow trees and throw our tears in the sea"

Words I repeat in my mind whenever I have the urge to hurt myself
I remember my past in moments of impact
A punch
A cut
A kiss
They all make me into who I am
Some moments feel better than others
But that's what this world is about
You can't dwell on them
So take a moment
Turn it into a memory
And keep going

If God were a woman

I sit on my floor next to my heart
Knees to chest
Arms wrapped around them
And I can feel my pulse in my finger tips
I gave myself to another person
And I can't get the feeling of the weight of his body on top of me off of me
I'm holding on to both of our weights so strongly
I feel the ground beneath me crack
I have learned to keep my nails cut short
So that I don't scratch my own eyes out
Trusting someone who you find out just wanted to make your body theirs for a night
Twists your brain into the shape of a question mark
And pulses in your mind
Why?
Why couldn't you use your own body for pleasure?
Why did you have to waste mine
On your own selfish touch
I wish getting your body back was as easy as giving it away
But it isn't
So I pray for the strength to carry the weight of his body
Along with the others on my back
For the rest of my life
And I believe that if God were a woman
This wouldn't feel so heavy
I think about this as the realization
That no boy has ever not in some way used me for

themselves
But what does it say about me that I have laid there each time
Continuously watching them take it
So I stay sitting on the floor
Reliving every moment I've ever wanted to disappear
And with each exhale I feel myself becoming smaller
Until I am as flat as the rug that they use to walk all over me
For the rest of my forever

Overflowing sink

My mind is an overflowing sink
Every time I turn the faucet on
To wash my hands clean from your touch
It only makes the water spill over the edge onto the floor
Soaking my shoes
I am trying to wash you away
But the more I try the more water spills out
All I need to do is reach in and pull out the plug
But then all I have left of you will circle the drain
And then how will I get my hands wet?
We've gone years without a word spoken between us
So what am I holding on to?
We don't exist in each other's lives anymore
and every day I walk further away from you
But I can only go so far
Before I realize I forgot the sound of your voice saying my name
So I walk backwards until I can hear it again
But the closer I get back to you
The harder it is for me to hear myself tell myself I love you
The more of you means less of me
And so every day I will take a step away
And when I can't hear your voice anymore
I will listen to my own
Mychaela keep walking
Mychaela you are okay
Mychaela I love you

White knuckling

My hands are bleeding from my nails digging into my palms
I've been white knuckling it for I don't even know how long
I've been stuck in this cycle for weeks now
And I feel it taking its toll
My eyes are dark
My skin is peeling
And my mind wanders to images of blood
Something I haven't thought about for awhile now
I'm slipping
And I don't want to slip
But I also know I can't stay like this
I can't stay just existing
When I try I can't remember the last time I lived
Really lived
And I keep thinking
Have I just been existing my whole life?

Don't cry

Last night I talked about you
And I didn't cry
For the first time in three years
I didn't cry
And I'm sitting here thinking about the night it all started
How you told me you had feelings for me
And I am not crying
It's a lonely feeling
Like I've been far away from home for days

Trying

I told myself I could always stop
That I could turn it off
But looking at this fool you made me
I don't know how to turn that off
I have a lot of regrets about the way you chose to see me
I left no trace of myself in your life
Not even a pair of socks as proof that I existed
No proof that I existed
And I knew I was ruining myself
Gasping for air
For the same air you breathed
But by the time I inhaled you exhaled any trace of yourself from my life
And it kills me every day that you trained your mind
To throw out any thought or memory not just of us as a couple
But of me as a person you once touched every day
I still struggle with days that I crave having your hand in mine
And I feel stupid
Because there was a time I told myself to turn it off
And now it's too late
And I can't stop
So this is me trying to end this
Once and for all
And I am really trying

Something perfect

We are not the same
We never were
And we were never going to be
I remember this one time
Sitting in the passenger seat of your car
You were holding my hand like you always did when you were driving
I remember looking down at your arm
It was perfect
An arm that has never felt the sting of a razor
Or the pinch of a tattoo gun
I looked down at my own arm
It looked so beat up next to yours
I have taken a razor to my arm
And it left its mark
Lines I will carry with me my whole life
I can still see them even with a tattoo over them
Sometimes I catch myself wanting to hold your hand
So that I can see your arm again
I just want to see something that hasn't tarnished
Something perfect

Words filling my mouth

Sometimes I feel like I never have anything to say
Like you plucked every opinion I would ever have out of my mind
Leaving me blank
When we were together I wanted all of my opinions to match yours
I never wanted to disagree
And if I did not agree with you
I learned how to hide the look on my face
When the words would slide up my throat into my mouth
And beat on the back of my lips
Trying their hardest to get out
I learned to swallow them like spit
I could hide it so well you never once questioned it
And even if you did
You didn't care enough to question the slight half second pause I took
Before agreeing with you
And just so you know I am not republican
And no it wasn't okay that you got drunk and forgot to call
The way you treated me was not right
And lastly
I am not ashamed of how much I loved you
Because at least I have proof that I know how to love someone
With everything I have
You will never be able to say that

I am learning to not hold in my thoughts
It will only bloat you beyond recognition
Words no matter how small should be spoken
And if you were standing in front of me today
And the words swelled up in my throat
Filling my mouth
Beating on the back of my lips
I would not swallow them
Instead I would spit them out all over you

He is pain

A prayer repeated for a year I never thought was answered
Lord I can't lose him
Please let him look me in the eyes and see his future
Let me be the one to change his outlook on life
God please
This will kill me
And I don't want to die
I just want to stop hurting
I love him but this hurts so bad
I want him with everything in me
Just take the pain away.
I looked in the mirror one night after a shower
I cried and said this prayer over and over again
Until the hot water turned cold
And I whispered to myself words I don't think were mine
"He is the pain"

Blood on your hands

One day when you're driving
And your windshield fills with rain one drop at a time
Until it's beating down so hard you can barely see
I hope you know that it's every tear I've ever cried over you
When the wind blows hard
And you can hear it slamming against your windows in your empty house
I hope you know that's all the wind you ever knocked out of me
And when it's the middle of the night and you're dreaming of nothing in particular
And you look down at your hands and they are full of blood
Just know that is my blood on your hands
Forever staining them red
For every cut I made on my body
For every time you made me feel like I was nothing but another conquest
I wish you love almost as much as I wish you hate
And of course I wish you happiness
But not without more sadness
And on the days I want you back
It's only so I can push you away
Far away
I wish you a full life
As well as an untimely demise
I hope the thought of me becomes something you crave

But can never reach
I don't need well wishes from you
And I don't crave your smile
And I don't need you to almost love me
As of today
The only love I wish for comes from a deep place in my heart
A heart that I can almost
Finally feel

Therapy

I think the reason I feel so dead inside now
Is because when I knew you
All I was living for
Was the hope that you would look me in the eyes and decide that it was enough
I was living for the hope that you would see me as a soft place to land
'I was living for the hope of it all to work out
To say you were my whole world
Doesn't quite reach the extent of how I felt about you
Everything in me is sinking so far down
And I've been floating just above the surface for so long
That I can't remember how to swim out of it
There are some things you can't talk about
And what happened to me after we ended is one of those things
But it is suffocating me
I need to get it out
So I pay a stranger to sit in a room with me
And listen to me talk in circles about how bad you hurt me
But still when the hour is up
It's like I didn't really say anything
Like I'll never have the words
I have done all the necessary things
I've taken the meds
I've gone to therapy
I have looked at myself in the mirror each morning and

decided to stay
So when will this all finally drain out of me?
I wasn't enough for him because I'm not enough for myself
So when does the lesson learned unveil itself?

Breathe

For the longest time I kept breathing for you
But you are also the reason I hold my breath
Sometimes until my lips turn blue.

Hospital stay

Waking up in a mental hospital
Is like realizing the nightmare you were just having has come to life
Windows with bars
Bed bolted to the floor
Nothing on the beige water-stained walls
I am alone
And I am scared
I try to soothe myself by counting the red flashes of the security camera
In the upper corner of the room
All I repeat to myself is
"Just go to sleep, you won't be scared if you're asleep"
But I dream of the empty room
And the cuts on my arm opening up
And filling the room with red
And again
I am scared
You don't realize how much home feels like home
Until you're far away for awhile
when I slept all the sleep out of me that I possibly could
I laid in bed and flashes of myself as a little girl come to mind
Giggling and swinging on the swing set in the backyard of my home
Flashes of watching myself growing up happy
My first softball game that I pitched a no hitter at the age of eleven

The first time my mother bought me makeup for my freshman year of high school
My first date with a boy I had no business dating
Watching my brother get his heart broken by a girl he will never stop loving
And going to prom with him and a beautiful girl with haunted eyes
That didn't live past twenty
Meeting you for the first time
Knowing you were going to have a huge impact on me
But not knowing it will coast me to lose all of who all these things made me to be
How did I get here?
Where did I go?
And will I ever come back?
That was the first time I cried in mourning of the person I destroyed
In the process of trying to love you
While I was crying myself back to sleep
I wondered when it got so hard to breathe
That was the first time I realized that I had been holding my breath
Since the first day you said my name
And no matter how hard I tried
I could not for the life of me
Exhale
A girl with a mane of hair suddenly appears in the doorway of my room
And at first I didn't know if she was real
All she said to me was
"If you want out of here fast, tell them all what they want

to hear"
Then just like that she was gone
That night I asked to take a shower
And when the nurse smiled I knew what that girl had said was true
So for four days I did everything suggested
And I said all the right things
I tried so hard to look like the model patient
And it worked
I just knew I had to get out
You were on my mind on mute all day
When night time came that was when the flashes of my life would start
But I didn't cry
I told myself I was healed
And when they let me out I didn't cry for two months
I also didn't laugh
Because nothing felt sad but nothing was funny anymore either
Feeling nothing was better than feeling everything
I started smoking
I said it was to curve my anxiety
Really it was just something I knew would take minutes off my life
And that was a comforting thought
I thought I was outsmarting the world
Until the thoughts of hurting myself came flooding back
You cannot outsmart your own mind
Trying to go back to my regular life
While pretending that I was completely okay was exhausting

But I fooled you
Only because you didn't care enough to lift the mask off of my face
And see that underneath my eyes were pleading, begging for help
You never learned to read my mind
Even though every thought spelled itself out across my eyes
But you never liked to read
You broke my heart every time you laughed while I was breaking inside
At times I wished I could go back to the hospital
So I could lay in that bed and have a clear picture of that little girl
On the swing, giggling away before the world turned ugly
Before she ever had an intrusive thought
Before I had to learn how to untangle you from me
Five years later I still want her back
And five years later
You're gone and I'm still here
That counts for something
It has to.

Indifference

I have this fear that you're going to die
Before I've learned to become indifferent to you
I'm afraid to be permanently tied to you
Through the love I have for you.

What to write

Whenever I don't know what to write
And I stare at the blank page
All the wrong I did
And hurt I caused the people
That I would kill for if it meant they would never feel hurt again
Comes flooding into my mind
I think about the look in their eyes
When I say the last thing they want to hear
The day I looked my mother straight in the eyes
And told her I didn't want to be alive
She spent nineteen years
Filling me with love and light
Making sure I was safe
And that I had a childhood of laughter
And I wanted to throw all of it away for a spot six feet underground
And I don't know how to apologize for that
When I'm aware of it
Yet I still have daydreams of a place I can only get to through death
She is the reason I stay above ground
I think of the very faint deep breath my brothers take
Holding it when they ask me how I'm doing
And the exhale of relief
when I'm able to smile and say things are getting better
I think about the relationship with my father
That has not been the same since mental illness took over

my life
Sometimes I think I've disappointed him with the way my life has played out
But some people just don't know how to talk to you
After you've almost ripped your life away from this earth
Before it was really your time to go
I relive breaking that boy's heart
Because I wanted someone else to give me the love he was handing me
Sometimes I want to write him a letter
But I don't know how to apologize without sounding like my behavior was excusable
I think about these things and suddenly the page isn't blank anymore
But I am somehow left
With more regret filling inside of me
Than what I started off with.

Time

I don't know what it feels like
To be in a long-lasting relationship without breaking up
Every relationship I've been in
Feels like we're running out of time
Before we even begin.

You don't have a heart anymore

I am willing to say that it is my fault
For letting myself fall so deeply for you
I chose to
And I need to take responsibility for how horribly this heartache hurts
But it hurts too much to just be pain from one heart
And that's how I know that you gave me your heart
Not for me to hold and love
But for me to carry for you
So you wouldn't have to feel any of this.

One last goodbye

I no longer feel the urge to scream your name into the wind at the top of a cliff
I no longer wish for you on every eyelash that falls to my cheek
I do not breathe life into the thought of us ending up together
My heart beats for no one but myself
I find myself slowly forgetting the uneasy feeling of loving you
There is still a spot in my soul that you took over
And it will never go away
I will always have a twinge of pain deep inside whenever something happens
And I turn to tell you but you're not there.
Sometimes I think all of this would be easier if you had died
Because the thought that you still exist
Living a life with someone else
After the agony I have gone through for years trying to get over you
Makes it that much harder to run away from
I wish that there was a final resting place
Where I can leave it all
Somewhere to go when I'm sad
Because I thought of a memory yesterday
A sweet memory
You were smiling and talking to me like I was the only person left in the world

I don't even know what we were talking about
But the way your eyes filled with joy when you looked at me
I wanted to live in this memory
At least for awhile
At least until I could feel it again
I had nowhere to leave it
So it's just floating around in my mind with all the other ones
No matter how hard I try
I don't know where to put them
And so I bury them
The way they would bury you in the ground
I bury it six feet deep inside me
And I cover it with the seal of our last kiss
I still don't have answers for why you did what you did to me
Or why you treated me like I was nothing
When you were my everything and then some
I am learning to be content with the fact
That not every question has an answer
You can love someone with every fiber of your being
That doesn't mean they have to love you back
And so I will take all that love I felt for you
And I will begin to pour it back into myself
When I stand on a cliff I will whisper my own name
With every eyelash
There will be a new wish without you in it
I breathe life back into myself in order to keep my own heart beating
You broke me

But I will no longer stand still
Waiting for you to fix me
It's time to start walking forward
I will leave you on these pages where you will stay
I know I'll come back and read it again
But when the words come to an end
The book will close
And I will do the same.

You weren't meant to stay broken.

www.ingramcontent.com/pod-product-compliance
Lightning Source LLC
LaVergne TN
LVHW091601060526
838200LV00036B/936